Canadian Social Studies (
Teacher Tips

Encouraging Topic Interest

Help students to develop an understanding and appreciation of different social studies concepts. Engage students through stories, non-fiction, easy- to- read books, videos, and other resources as a springboard for learning.

Vocabulary List

Students can use the black line master to record new vocabulary of theme related words. In addition, keep track of new and theme related vocabulary on chart paper for students' reference during writing activities. Encourage students to add theme related words. Classify the word list into the categories of nouns, verbs and adjectives.

Black Line Masters and Graphic Organizers

Use the black line masters and graphic organizers to present information, reinforce important concepts and to extend opportunities for learning. The graphic organizers will help students focus on important ideas, or make direct comparisons.

Learning Logs

Keeping a learning log is an effective way for students to organize their thoughts and ideas about the social studies concepts presented. Student learning logs also give the teacher insight on what follow up activities are needed to review and to clarify concepts learned.

Learning logs can include the following kinds of entries:
- Teacher prompts
- Student personal reflections
- Questions that arise
- Connections discovered
- Labeled diagrams and pictures

Rubrics and Checklists

Use the rubrics and checklists in this book to assess student learning.

Table of Contents

Families

Activity 1: What is a family?

In a whole group setting, brainstorm with students about what makes up a family. Some families may be traditional nuclear families, extended families, single-parent families, blended families, foster families, or same-sex families.

On a web graphic organizer, model how you are in the middle with different family members around you. Explain your relationship to each family member. For example:

- My mother is my family because I am her daughter/son.
- My brother is my family because we share the same parents/father, and/or mother.

The teacher may wish to showcase a different student's family each day. Invite families to send in pictures and to complete questions about their family life and favourite memories.

Activity 2: Family Trees

Show students how families differ in size and make-up by creating individual family trees.

1. First, model for students how to trace their hand onto green construction paper and how to carefully cut it out.
2. Have students then cut out a hand for each member of their family.
3. Next, have students write a family member name on each hand shape. Each hand shape with a family member name will represent a leaf on their family tree.
4. On a piece of paper have students use brown crayon to draw the trunk of their family tree.
5. Demonstrate for students how to place and glue on their family member leaves onto their tree trunk.

Discussion Questions:
- How are the family trees the same or different?

Activity 3: Class Graphing Ideas

Show students how people can be similar and/or different by surveying students to create class bar graphs about:

- birthday months
- number of people in their household
- favourite colours
- favourite foods
- number of siblings
- eye or hair colour

Discussion questions:

1. What do they notice?

2. What was the most common answer?

3. What was the least common answer?

Rules and Responsibilities

Activity 1: Families Work Together

As a whole group, ask students if they think families are important and to explain their thinking with examples. Then ask children to think about special contributions each family member makes to the family. Record the student responses on a chart. Put checkmarks or tally marks to show repeat answers. Encourage students to think about their own role in their family. What do they contribute? How is it helpful to the family?

Give students a family chart to take home and record how their family works together.

Activity 2: Rules and Responsibilities at Home

As a whole group, brainstorm different rules that students have at home. List the different rules on a chart and poll the students if they have each rule at their home. Some of the rules that might be stated are: I have a bedtime, I am not allowed to go near the stove without an adult, I need to be polite, I need to tidy up my toys, etc.

Discussion Starters:

1. Which rules keep you safe at home?

2. Which rules help keep you healthy?

3. Which rules help the members of your family to get along?

4. What do you think would happen if you didn't have any rules at home?

5. What rules would you change? Why?

Activity 3: Rules and Responsibilities at School

Using paper strips, have the students brainstorm classroom or school rules together. Some rules might include: Walk in the hallways, keep your hands to yourself, be polite, ask permission to go to the bathroom etc.

Discussion Starters:

1. Ask the students which rule they feel is the most important.

2. Who do you think should make up the rules in the classroom or at school? Explain your thinking.

3. Which rules help keep you safe?

4. Which rules help you learn?

5. What are your responsibilities at school?

6. What are the responsibilities of the people who work at your school?

5. Are there different rules for inside the school and outside the school?

Activity 4: Rules in Public Places

Do the same as above, but while talking about public places.

All About My Family

Dear Families,

As part of our social studies focus on families, please complete the following handouts for your child to share with their classmates. In addition, families are welcome to send in photographs or other special artifacts.

Your participation is greatly appreciated!

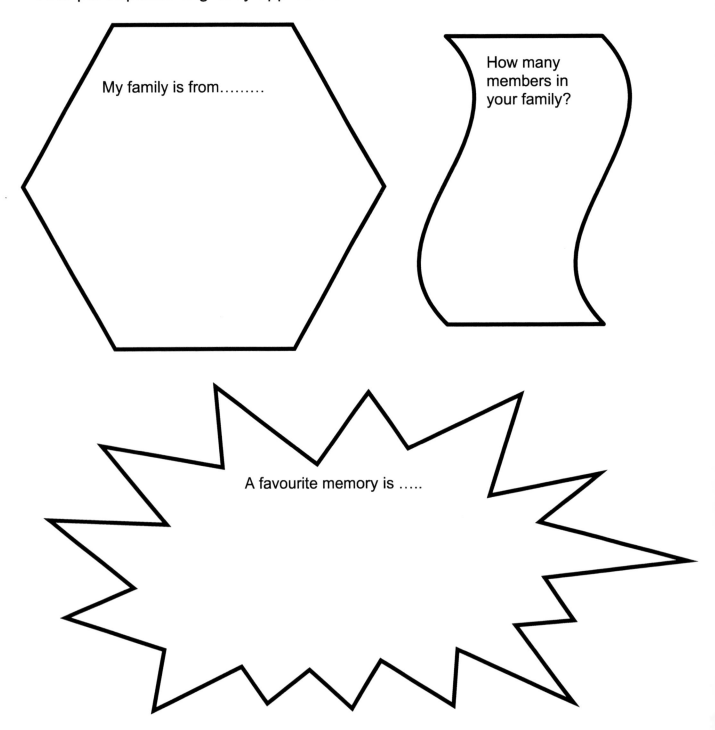

My family is from………

How many members in your family?

A favourite memory is …..

name _____

This is a picture of my family.

My family is special because.....

_____

A Family Stamp

name _____

Create a family stamp to show something your family enjoys doing together.

Write about your stamp.

_____

_____

My name is _____

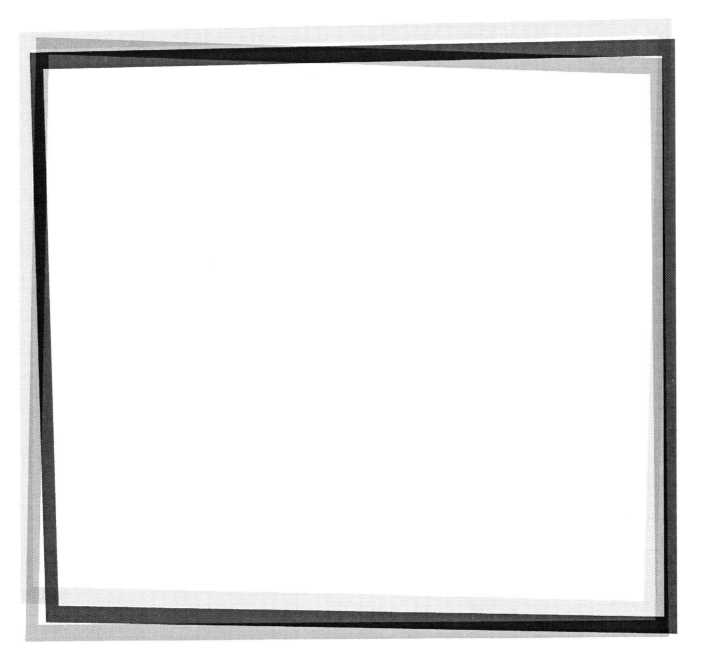

I am _____ years old.

My favourite thing to do is _____.

My favourite food is _____.

I am special because _____

_____.

Family Members Work Together   name _____

Please fill out this chart to help your child develop an understanding of how families function and how various family members contribute. For example sister, - helps feed the baby. Parents- cook meals. Encourage your child to think about their own role in your family. What do they contribute? How do they help?

Family Member	Job or Contribution

Changes In Your Life

name _____

In the chart below, identify a change in your life.
An example might be moving to another place or getting a new pet.

What was a change in your life?

What happened after the change?

How did you feel about the change?

How I Have Changed

	When I was little	Now
My size		
The food I eat		
The toys I like to play with		
Where I sleep		

Someone Special

This is a picture of someone special in my life.

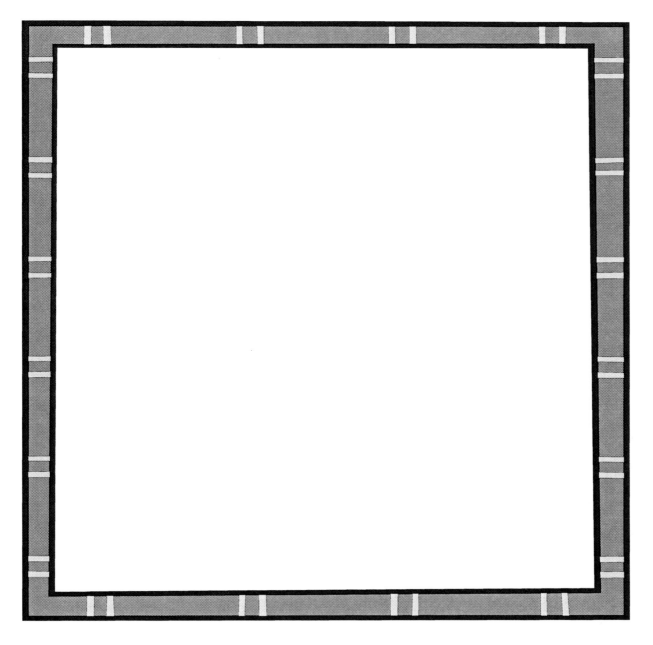

_____ is special to me because…

_____

_____

An important event in my life was:

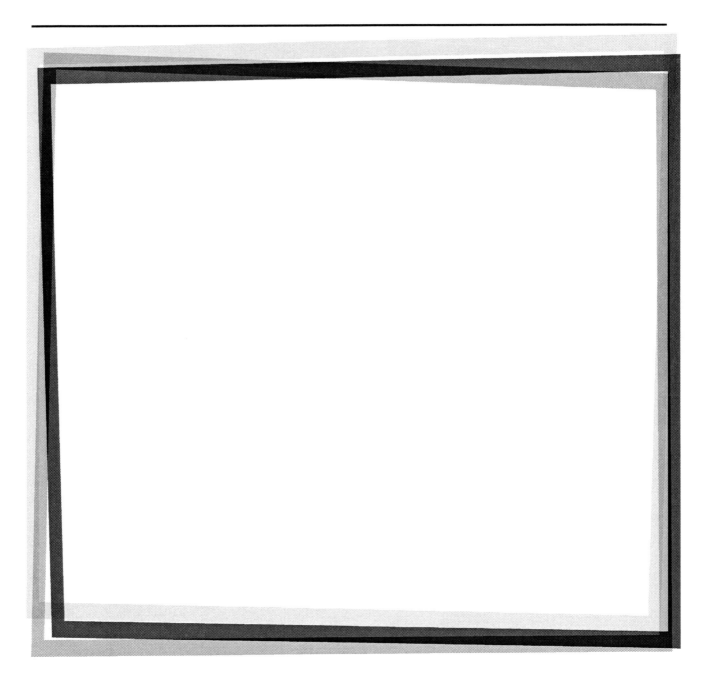

This was important because _____

_____

_____

_____

A rule at_____is
_____

_____

This rule is important because _____

_____

_____

_____

A Time Line

name _____

Age	Important Event

A day in the life of _____

Time Of Day	What Happens?

Daily Activities

Use the cards to make a timeline of your day.

Breakfast	Lunch
School Time	School Time
Lesson	Dinner
Play Time	Play Time
Get Ready For School	Get Ready For Bed Time
Snack	Get Ready For School

Our Community Activities

Help students develop an understanding and appreciation for their local community. Engage students through oral stories, neighbourhood walks, non-fiction easy to read books, videos, maps, class speakers, community artifacts, and other resources as a springboard for learning.

Activity Idea 1: People Live In Communities

In a whole group, introduce students to the idea that a community is a place where people live, work, and share the same interests. Communities can be small or very large.

Discussion Starters:
- What size is your community?
- What makes your community special?

Activity Idea 2: Make a Class Community Scrap Book

As the class learns about their community, create an ongoing community scrapbook. The teacher may wish to use chart paper or large poster board to make the scrapbook oversized. For each page write a class paragraph and then paste on pictures, or other memorabilia from the community, such as flyers, announcements, postcards, etc.

Headings may include:
- Our Community Is Special
- People Who Live In Our Community
- Community Workers
- People- At- Work
- Physical Features
- Buildings In Our Community
- Transportation In Our Community
- Public Places

Activity Idea 3: People- At- Work Cards

As students learn about different people in the community and their jobs, include examples of women and men working in nontraditional ways.

Use the people -at- work cards in various ways.

1) Have students pick a card and talk about what they do and what tools they use in their job. The other students have to guess who they are.
2) Make two sets of the people at work cards and have students use them to play a game of concentration.

Use the people at work cards to classify and sort different types of jobs.

For example:
- work in stores
- help us
- work in factories
- work in offices
- help keep us safe
- help us learn

The profiles may be displayed in a big book, on a bulletin board, as mobiles hung from the ceiling, or on small display boards set on tables.

Our Community Activities

Activity Idea 4: Community Drama Centres

Have students bring in items that represent places in the community, and to role play what happens there.

Post Office – Create a class mailbox and provide items like stamps, stationary and envelopes. Have students write letters or postcards to each other. Assign a postal worker to deliver class mail.

Hospital – Provide a play medical kit and medical masks. Students can role play a doctor, nurse and patient.

Store – Create a store based on what they want to sell, provide play money, receipt papers for store owners and customers. Students may bring in empty packages, cans or other items for the store. Use stickers for price tags.

Restaurant – Provide a table, chairs, plastic cutlery, paper cups, plates, and plastic food. Students can role play a waiter/waitress, chef, or customers. Students can design menus for the restaurant. Provide play money, receipt papers for restaurant owners and customers

Grocery Store – Have students bring in empty cans, cereal boxes, juice boxes, etc. Use stickers as price tags on items for students to "buy". Provide play money, receipt papers for cashiers and customers. Students can role play a shopper, grocery stackers, and cashier. Students may also create daily sale posters.

Activity Idea 5: Community Public Places

Go on a field trip to the grocery store, fire hall, police station, mall, or bank. Plan visits to various work places in the community, such as the fire hall, police station, a bakery, library, radio station, newspaper, book store, machine shop, lumber yard, etc.

The visits may be done as a whole group or, if there are enough parent volunteers, the class may be divided to visit different places. Other ideas include:

- Have students interview employees or managers about their work.
- Have students keep track of man-made things vs. natural things.

If possible, before the visit, use books and videos to study the workplaces that will be visited. If resources are not available, discuss what the students expect to see and experience. Discuss possible questions they might ask.

Activity Idea 6: Animal Life Found In The Community

As a whole group, small group or individually, make a chart or complete a graphic organizer that tells about the animals that live in your community. Classify animals as tame or wild.

When I Grow Up

name _____

When I grow up I want to be _____.

The reason is …..

_____

_____

People- At- Work Cards

construction worker

fisherman

police officer

veterinarian

hair stylist

fireman

People- At -Work Cards

farmer

city worker

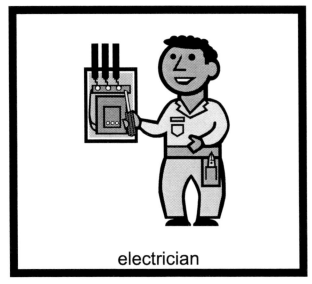

electrician

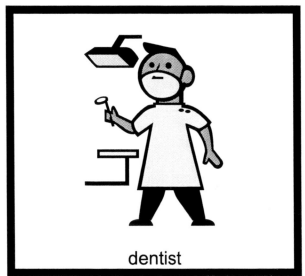

dentist

politician

landscaper

People- At -Work Cards

office worker

restaurant worker

florist

sanitation worker

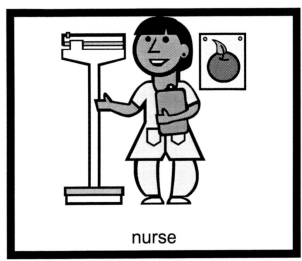

nurse

teacher

People- At -Work Cards

tailor

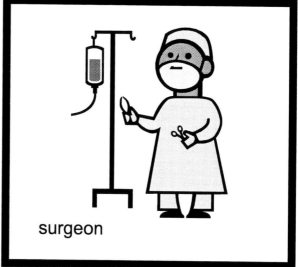

surgeon

brick layer

artist

business person

television worker

People- At -Work Cards

crossing guard

teacher

painter

scientist

life guard

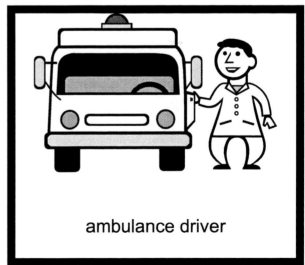

ambulance driver

People- At- Work Cards

actor

miner

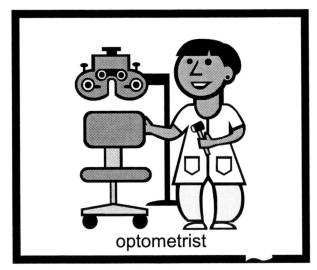

optometrist

farmer

bee keeper

house keeper

People- At -Work Cards

plumber

baker

judge

postal worker

librarian

architect

Community Helpers

What kind of community helper would you want to be?

_____

Draw a picture.

I would want to be this community helper because:

_____

A special tool or piece of equipment that this community helper uses is:

_____

Community Workers: Fire Fighters

name _____

Fire fighters are community workers. They help keep us safe by putting out fires, or helping us with other emergencies. Some of the special tools and pieces of equipment that fire fighters use are a helmet, face mask, jacket, pants, boots, gloves, ax, and water hose.

Colour the picture and add details.

Fill in the blanks using information from the reading.

1) Fire fighters are _____ workers.

2) They help keep us safe by putting out _____.

3) Two of the special tools and pieces of equipment that

fire fighters use are _____ and _____.

van

scooter

train

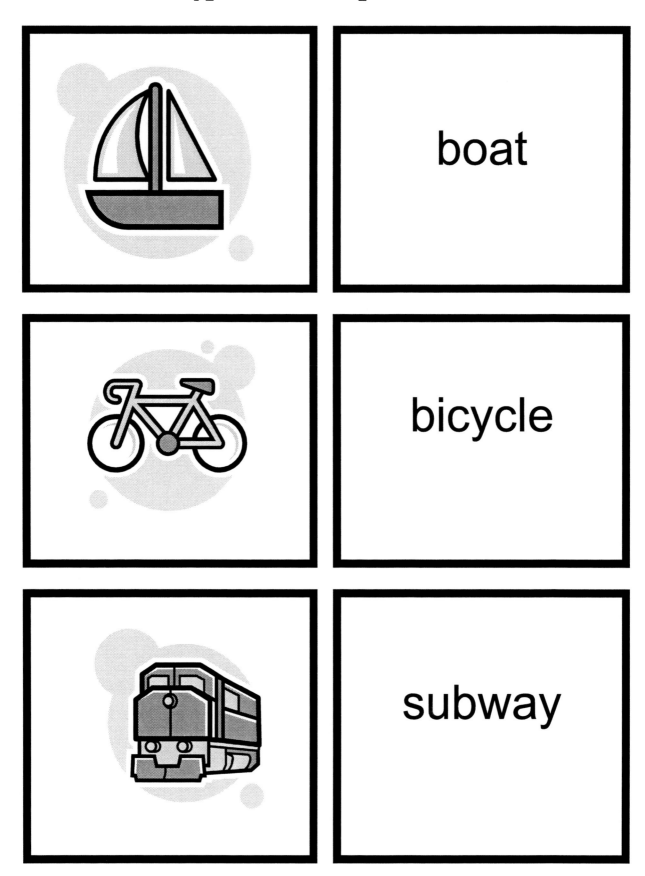

boat

bicycle

subway

car

bus

helicopter

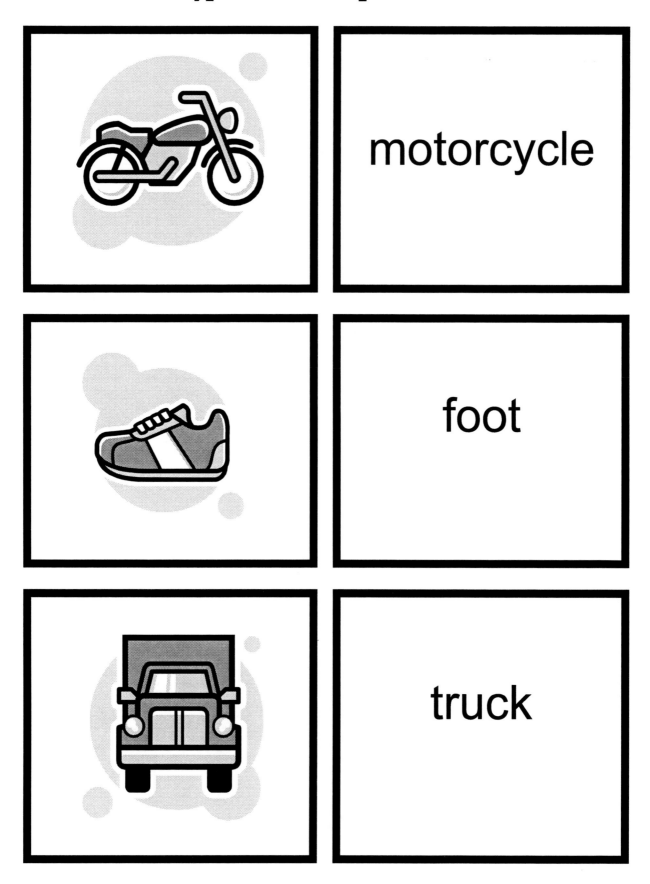

Transportation Survey

name _____

What kind of transportation links do you use? Conduct a survey of your classmates and tally the results.

Type of Transportation	Tally Marks
Walk	
Bicycle	
School bus	
Public Bus	
Subway	
Train	
Car	
Airplane	
Other	

What is the most popular method of transportation? _____

How do you think your community's natural environment affects transportation used by people? Explain your thinking.

Our Community Book

name _____

This is a picture of _____

This person, place or thing is important to the community because:

_____

_____

Our Community: Public Places

Communities have public places. Public places are where people can get together to play, like a park; learn, like a library; or be entertained, like at a movie theatre.

Draw a picture of your favourite public place.

My favourite public place is_____

because _____

_____

_____

Community Walk

A community is a place where people live, work, and share the same interests.

By _____

Draw and label the different kinds of homes found in your community.

Circle the ways people travel around your community.

van   scooter   train   boat

bicycle   subway   Foot   truck

car   bus   helicopter   airplane

Other _____

What is your favourite way to travel? _____

Draw a public place people go to have fun in your community.

What kinds of street signs do you see in your community?

What businesses are in your community?

I think people choose to live in our community because…

Some physical features of our community are…

T-Shirt Design

Create an important message or slogan about your community.

What is your T-Shirt about?

Urban and Rural Communities

Activity Idea 1: Understanding Needs and Wants

In a whole group, ask students what they think they need in order to survive. Next, ask students what things they want, but don't need in order to survive. As a class, come up with a definition for needs and wants.

Needs are things that people must have to survive. For example: food and water, clothing, and shelter.

Wants are things that people would like, but don't need to survive. For example: computer, toys, refrigerator.

Discussion Starters:

1) Where do you go into the community to meet your needs?

2) Where do you go into the community to meet your wants?

Activity Idea 2: Community Pen Pals

Encourage students to get to know their peers in communities across Canada.
Have each student in the class write to another child in the same grade, from a different province or territory. Write about where they are from, facts about their community and aspects of their daily life. Add pictures and questions for the other child. Your class may also want to be involved in the following project.

Activity Idea 3: Community Brochure

Have students pretend that they are going on a vacation in another community such as one of the provincial capital cities. Have students choose two communities they would want to visit. Students choose topics to write about the communities in the form of a brochure.

- Where is the community located?
- What are the physical features?
- Why would you want to go there?
- What would you do?
- What are some interesting facts about that community?

Here is a link to provincial websites that will help you find a community to visit.
http://canada.gc.ca/othergov/prov_e.html

Here is a link to provincial capital cities websites.
http://www.capitaleducanada.gc.ca/ccco/index_e.asp

Activity Idea 4:

Use the various graphic organizers to compare urban and rural communities.

Great Websites To Learn About Communities

http://atlas.gc.ca/site/english/learningresources/ccatlas/index.html

The Canadian Communities Atlas offers a unique national network of geographic information by providing schools the opportunity to create an internet-based atlas of their community.

http://www.ext.vt.edu/resources/4h/virtualfarm/main.html

This is an excellent website for students to explore different kinds of farming. By exploring this website students will gain a better understanding of how farming affects their daily lives.

http://www.whitebirch.ca/kids/kids.shtml

This is a great website sponsored by the Saskatchewan Forestry Association. This site provides interesting information about forestry and has a special section for kids.

http://www.epa.gov/recyclecity/

This is a great interactive website for students to learn about recycling at Recycle City.

http://www.aboriginalcanada.com/firstnation/

This is an informative website that allows you to navigate through a directory of several First Nations community websites.

http://www.lizardpoint.com/fun/geoquiz/canquiz.html

This is fun website where students can test their knowledge of where provinces and territories are located on a map.

http://ceps.statcan.ca/english/profil/placesearchform1.cfm

This government website allows students to find out information about communities across Canada. A mapping feature is also available.

http://www.econedlink.org/lessons/index.cfm?lesson=EM194

This website is sponsored by the National Council on Economic Education in the United States. This webpage allows students to take part in interactive lessons on the types of goods or services that businesses offer.

http://pbskids.org/rogers/

The Mister Rogers Neighourhood website has sections where kids can build their own neighbourhood or take a factory tour to see how things are made.

http://www.nrcan.gc.ca/mms/wealth/intro-e.htm

This government website allows students to take a tour of spaces in the home and identifies minerals used in many household items.

Urban and Rural Communities

name _____

A **community** is a place where people live, work, and share the same interests. When people live in a **village**, **reserve** or **hamlet,** it is called a **rural community**. When people live in a **town**, **city** or **suburb,** their community is called an **urban community**. Some communities are smaller like the town of Fox Creek, Alberta. Some communities are very large like the city of Toronto, Ontario.

Rural Communities

Rural communities are usually small and have less traffic than towns or cities. People usually live spread out from each other and there is a lot of open space. Some people in rural communities work in jobs related to farming, forestry, mining or fishing.

Urban Communities

Urban communities usually have lots of people, buildings, stores, and traffic. People usually live near each other in houses, duplexes or apartment buildings.

Brain Stretch:

Using information from the reading and your own ideas, explain the kind of community you live in.

_____

_____

_____

_____

_____

_____

_____

A Community Profile

Community Name _____

Location of Community	
What kind of community is it?	
What natural resources or physical features are there?	
What are some of the types of jobs that people might have in this community?	
What kinds of things do people do for fun in this community for fun?	
What are some interesting facts about this community?	

The Features of a Community   name _____

Community Name _____

Location of Community	
What kind of community is it?	
What natural resources or physical features are there?	
How are the land and natural resources used?	
What kinds of structures are in this community?	
What kind of transportation is available in this community?	

A Community Collage

name _____

Create a community collage. Search through magazines, brochures, or newspapers to find people, places, things or words that remind you of your community. Cut and paste these pictures into a collage in the space below or on a separate piece of paper.

Write about your collage.

_____

_____

_____

_____

_____

CANADIAN FARMING COMMUNITIES

Canada has many farming communities. Usually, neighbours in a farming community live quite a distance from each other. Stores, hospitals, or places to sell crops are usually located in a nearby town. Sometimes a farming community includes a town and the farms that surround the town. Canada has many types of farms such as dairy, vegetable, cattle, poultry, fruit, and fish.

To learn more about different kinds of farming and how farming affects our daily lives, go the following website.

http://www.ext.vt.edu/resources/4h/virtualfarm/main.html

Brain Stretch:

- What kind of farm would you like to have? Explain your thinking.
- How do you think farming communities are important to people who live in other communities? Explain your thinking.

MINING COMMUNITIES

Canada has many mining communities. Mining is the removal of minerals and metals from the earth. Some types of mines in Canada include gold, silver, zinc, nickel, lime, salt, and others. Most people who live in a mining community work for the mining company in some way such as in the mine, in the mining offices or the company cafeteria.

Go to this website to find out where there are mining communities in Canada.

http://mmsd1.mms.nrcan.gc.ca/mmsd/producers/default_e.asp

Take a tour and identify how minerals are used in many household items.
http://www.nrcan.gc.ca/mms/wealth/intro-e.htm

Brain Stretch:
- How do you think mining communities affect the daily lives of people in other communities? Explain your thinking.

MANUFACTURING COMMUNITIES

Many Canadians live in manufacturing communities. The word manufacture means to make a completed product using raw materials. Some examples of manufactured goods are: cars, televisions, furniture, food products, toys or bubble gum. Usually, in a manufacturing community people work at a factory or plant. Not all people at the plant work to build something, some people work at a plant or factory to supply services to other workers. These services include medical, social, security and food services.

Visit the following website to see how a factory produces bubble gum.

http://www.dubblebubble.com/tour.html

Brain Stretch:

- Why do you think there are so many different workers in a manufacturing community? Explain your thinking.
- How do you think manufacturing communities affect the lives of people in other communities? Explain your thinking.

FORESTRY COMMUNITIES

Some Canadians live in forestry communities. Forestry means the cutting down and replanting of trees. Trees are a natural resource that is used to make wood products such as paper or lumber for building. Usually people in a forestry community have jobs that are centred on forestry. One of the important jobs in a forestry community is the replanting of trees so that this natural resource does not run out.

Go to the kids' section of the Saskatchewan Forestry Association website to learn more.

http://www.whitebirch.ca/kids/kids.shtml

Brain Stretch:
- Using your ideas, explain why it is important to replant trees.
- How do you think forestry communities affect the lives of people in other communities?

PORT COMMUNITIES

Some Canadians live in port communities. A port is a harbour or place for ships to dock and unload. Port communities are important for the transfer of goods such as grains, mineral ore, and other products. They help transport these things from community to community. Some of this cargo is then delivered across Canada and other parts of North America by trains, trucks or airplanes. Well known Canadian port cities include: Montreal, Québec; Vancouver, British Columbia; Halifax, Nova Scotia; Québec City, Québec; St. John's, Newfoundland; and Churchill, Manitoba. Port cities can be found on the east coast, west coast, Hudson Bay and along the St. Lawrence River.

Visit this website to learn about the St. Lawrence Seaway system.
http://www.greatlakes-seaway.com/en/home.html

Brain Stretch:
- How do you think port communities affect the lives of people in other communities?

FISHING COMMUNITIES

Some Canadians live in fishing communities. Canada is home to the Great Lakes and has the world's longest coastline. Some fishing communities have large ports with transportation connections, large fish processing plants, shipyards, and fish research facilities. Other fishing communities are very small and have small anchorages where boats are pulled onto the beach.

The Canadian fisheries department decides how many fish can be caught. This is to prevent over fishing. When over fishing happens nature cannot replace all the fish that is caught, quickly enough. The Canadian government also protects the fishing industry by preventing other countries from fishing within 200 nautical miles of Canada's coast.

Learn more about Canada's oceans at this government website.
http://www.dfo-mpo.gc.ca/canwaters-eauxcan/bbb-lgb/index_e.asp

Brain Stretch:
- Make list of types of fish and seafood caught in Canada.
- How do you think fishing communities affect the lives of people in other communities?

CREATE AN URBAN COMMUNITY MAP

On grid paper, create a map of an urban community. Think about including things like:

❖ highways	❖ public places	❖ apartment buildings	❖ roads
❖ houses	❖ stores	❖ school	❖ hospital
❖ factory	❖ sanitation plant	❖ physical features	❖ government buildings

Brain Stretch:

- Why might people who live in a rural community like to visit an urban community? Explain your thinking.

- Complete a community profile to tell about your urban community.

CREATE A RURAL COMMUNITY MAP

On grid paper create a map of a rural community. Think about including things like:

❖ highway	❖ farms	❖ forest	❖ school
❖ houses	❖ farm fields	❖ school	❖ stores
❖ physical features	❖ orchards	❖ hospital	

Brain Stretch:

- Why might people who live in an urban community like to visit a rural community? Explain your thinking.

- Complete a community profile to tell about your rural community.

FIRST NATIONS COMMUNITIES

First Nations communities are located in both rural and urban areas across Canada. First Nations communities are called Indian reserves. An **Indian reserve** is land saved for the use of status Indians. **Status Indians** are people who are registered under the Indian Act.

Each First Nations community is unique. There are big communities and there are small communities. Each community shows their nation's culture, traditions and language. Some First Nations communities are known for being a part of an industry like forestry or oil.

Visit the following website to learn about First Nations Communities.
http://www.aboriginalcanada.com/firstnation/

Brain Stretch:
- Why do you think it is important that each community show their nation's culture, traditions and language?

CITIES

Cities can be different sizes and change over time. People in cities usually live in houses, apartment buildings, townhouses, duplexes, or other buildings. Usually cities have some kind of industry, manufacturing, stores, government buildings, hospitals, museums, shopping malls, sports arenas, and schools. Each province has a capital city. The capital city of Canada is Ottawa, Ontario.

Go to the following website and learn more about Canada's provincial capital cities websites.
http://www.capitaleducanada.gc.ca/ccco/index_e.asp

Brain Stretch:

- In your opinion, why do you think people may prefer to live in a city instead of another kind of community?

Reasons for Living in an Urban Area	Reasons for Living in an Rural Area

Communities From Around The World

Help students to develop an understanding and appreciation of different countries around the world. Engage students through multicultural stories, non-fiction easy- to- read books, videos, and other resources as a springboard for learning.

Activity Idea 1: A Map Is A Flat Drawing Of Place

In a whole group setting, review with students how a map is a flat drawing of a place. Next, discuss with students how small things on a map represent large things in real life.

- With the guidance of the class, on chart paper draw a simple map of the classroom, or schoolyard. The teacher may wish to talk about how symbols are used to represent different things on maps.

- Then have students draw something of their own map of something like their bedroom.

Activity Idea 2: Globes and Maps

In a whole group setting, review with students what they know about a globe or world map. Brainstorm a list of types of information that people can get from these two things. Using a globe or world map have students find water and land.

Encourage students to notice that there is a world, and that:

- the world is made up of continents,

- those continents have countries within them

- those countries are divided up into smaller sections, such as provinces.

Challenge students by asking them to locate other countries, i.e.: where their families are from. The teacher may wish to keep track of the different countries by placing pins, or stars, etc. to mark locations.

Activity Idea 3: People Have Likenesses and Differences

Encourage students to realize that people can be alike and different. In a whole group setting play the *Just Like Me* game. Have students group themselves according to various criteria. For example:

- favourite ice cream flavour
- colour of hair
- birthday months
- colour of what they are wearing
- number of pets
- favourite books

Next, have students use the *Just Like Me* sheet to find students who are alike according to different criteria. Discuss as a whole group afterwards what they found out.

Activity Idea 4: Aspects of Different Countries

On an ongoing basis keep charts to focus on various aspects of lifestyles in different countries, like homes, school, roles of children and adults, recreation, celebrations, and natural features such as landscape, vegetation or climate. Students may then use the information on the charts to complete different graphic organizers.

Communities From Around the World

Activity 5: Class Graphing Ideas

Create whole class bar graphs to show students how people can be alike or different. Surveys may include:

- languages spoken
- number of people in their household
- food specialties
- favourite foods
- number of siblings
- eye or hair colour

Discussion Questions:

1. What do they notice?
2. What was the most or least popular?

Activity Idea 6: Food From Around The World

Invite students to bring in food items, food labels or pictures of food from around the world. Make a list of all the different items and where they are from.

Discussion Starters:

- Why do you think grocery stores have foods from other parts of the world?
- What are some foods you think that Canada grows or produces and sells to other countries?

The teacher may wish for each family in the class to contribute a recipe or a food sample from their culture. Bind the recipes into a booklet and make a copy for each student.

Activity Idea 7: Homes Found Around The World

In a whole group setting, ask students to brainstorm different kinds of homes. Answers may include: houses, semi detached houses, townhouses, apartments, mobile homes. Challenge students' thinking and ask what they would think it would be like to live on a boat, tent or not a home.

Other Activity Ideas:

1) Learn selected words or phrases from various languages. Display them in the classroom and use them at appropriate times.

2) Check out the weather from around the weather. Ask students how the weather affects the way they live and compare to other countries.

3) Each day, read a different version of a fairy tale from around the world. Chart the stories and discuss how the fairy tales are the same or different.

Great Websites About:
Traditions, Celebrations and
Countries From Around The World

http://www.cp-pc.ca/english/

This is a great website that gives summaries of life and customs of many countries at a primary reading level.

http://library.thinkquest.org/J0110166/hopscotch.htm

Introduce to students that a game can have different versions. The following website shows how hopscotch is played around the world.

http://www.dltk-kids.com/world/index.htm

Visit this website for information, crafts, colouring pages, recipes and other countries' cultures activities.

http://www.theholidayzone.com/main.html

At this website, holidays are listed and provide history of the holiday, activities, and language activities.

www.mamalisa.com/world/
At this website, you will find kids' songs from around the world with English translations or French Translations. Countries are listed in alphabetical order for easy look-up.

www.peacecorps.gov/**kids/world/**

Visit this website and explore a few of the Peace Corps' 70 countries around the globe. Click on the shaded regions of the world map, and learn interesting facts.

www.birthdaycelebrations.net/traditions.htm

Learn about birthday traditions from around the world. This is a very interesting site devoted to the celebration of birthdays including its origins.

http://www.topics-mag.com/internatl/holidays/festivals.htm

This website has an abundant amount of information about various holidays and festivals. This is site is excellent for research.

http://www.oxfam.org.uk/coolplanet/kidsweb/index.htm

Visit this website and explore the lives of children from different countries around the world.

http://www.kids-space.org/CTC/

Go to this website and learn about traditional costumes from around the world.

Just Like Me!

name_____

Someone who has the same birthday month as you.	Someone who has the same favourite food.	Someone who has the same colour hair.
Someone who lives on your street.	Someone who likes the same book as you do.	Someone who has likes the same kind of pet as you.
Someone who has the same favourite colour.	Someone who has the same favourite colour.	Someone who is in the same class as you.

Let's take a trip to:

_____

By _____

- -

Location of the country: _____

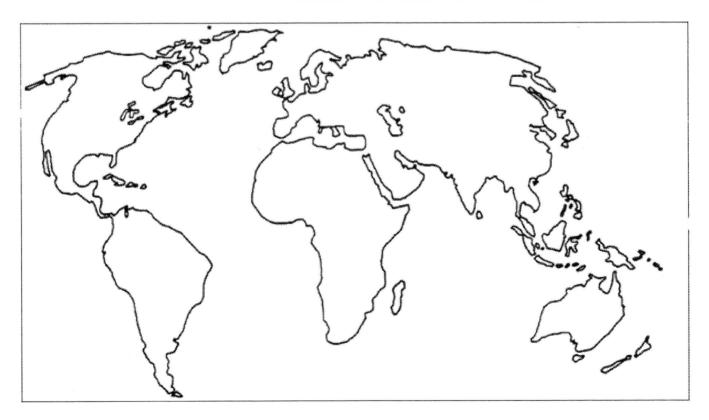

Climate

_____

_____

_____

Physical Features

_____

_____

_____

Languages Spoken

_____

_____

_____

Homes

_____

_____

_____

Food

_____

_____

_____

- -

Traditions / Celebrations

_____

_____

_____

Places To Visit

_____

_____

_____

- -

Things To Do

_____

_____

_____

Animals

_____

_____

_____

Interesting Facts

_____

_____

_____

Traditions and Celebrations Activities

Activity Idea 1: Why celebrate?

As a class, map the special days of the year with a timeline. Students can keep track of national holidays, make and use a timeline, and appreciate the unique nature and shared values of family celebrations.

- Make and display a monthly timeline that shows a full year.

- Mark Canadian holidays in red.

- Mark class birthdays in blue.

- Other multicultural holidays in green

- Mark special school days in orange.

Activity Idea 2: Show and Tell

Have students sign up for a special day to show and tell about their family's special tradition or celebration. Encourage students or their parents to:

- Bring in foods, symbol, music, decorations or special clothing that help mark a special celebration or tradition in their family

- Fill out a tradition and celebration sheet to explain their tradition or celebration

Activity Idea 3: Keep Ongoing Charts

As a whole group activity, chart information about the celebrations of various communities. Identify the origin and significance of each celebration. The teacher may choose to look at the ways certain celebrations are observed in different regions. Create art, learn songs and dances, and make foods related to some celebrations. Students may then use the information on the charts to complete different graphic organizers or other black line masters such as creating a stamp.

My Family's Traditions and Celebrations

By _____

- -

Tradition or Celebration

Describe a family tradition or celebration.

_____

_____

_____

Who Takes Part?

_____

_____

_____

— · — · — · — · — · — · — · — · — · — · — · — · — · — · — · — · — ·

When And Where?

_____

_____

_____

Special Food

_____

_____

_____

Special Outfits or Costumes

_____

_____

_____

Special Symbols

_____

_____

_____

- -

My Favourite Part

_____

_____

_____

A Tradition or Celebration

name _____

Name of tradition or celebration: _____

Why is it celebrated or recognized?	
What happens at the tradition or celebration?	
Who takes part?	
When does it take place?	
Where does it take place?	

Dates Of Special Days

name _____

Many Canadians celebrate the following days.
Mark the special days you celebrate on the chart below.

January 1st	New Year's Day
February 14th	St. Valentine's Day
February 15th	National Flag Day
March 17th	St. Patrick's Day
April 1st	April Fool's Day
May 24th	Victoria Day
July 1st	Canada Day
September 1st	Labour Day
October (second Monday)	Thanksgiving
October 31st	Halloween
November 1st	All Saints Day
December 25th	Christmas
December 26th	Boxing Day
December 31st	New Year's Eve

Many Canadian families celebrate traditions and celebrations that originated in their home country.

Make a list of other special days that students from your class celebrate.

_____

_____

_____

Canadian Community Celebrations and Festivals

Many Canadian communities have their own unique celebrations and festivals. Some celebrations are based on the community's heritage. Some celebrations are based on the type of food grown there. Community celebrations and festivals encourage people to be proud of where they live. Visit the following websites to learn more!

Community	Celebration or Festival	Events
Brighton, Ontario	Applefest http://www.applefest.reach.net/	baking contests, arts and crafts
Québec City, Québec	Carnaval De Québec http://www.carnaval.qc.ca/	winter carnival, ice sculptures, contests
Calgary, Alberta	Calgary Exhibition and Stampede http://calgarystampede.com/	wild west rodeo and stampede
Shediac, New Brunswick	Shediac Lobster Festival http://www.lobsterfestival.nb.ca/	celebrating "the lobster capital of the world"
St. John's, Newfoundland	Newfoundland and Labrador Folk Festival http://www.sjfac.nf.net/	a cultural showcase
Dawson City, Yukon	Dawson City Discovery Days http://www.dawsoncity.org/index.php	celebration of the Klondike gold discovery
Regina, Saskatchewan	Western Canada International Pow Wow	celebration of native crafts, and foods
Vancouver, British Columbia	Alcan Dragon Boat Festival http://www.adbf.com/	Chinese dragon boat races
Kentville, Nova Scotia	Annapolis Valley Apple Blossom Festival http://www.appleblossom.com/	parades, dances and sports and food activities
Bala, Ontario	Bala Cranberry Festival http://www.balacranberryfestival.on.ca/	marsh tours, midway rides, and arts and crafts

Does your community have a special celebration or festival? If so create a poster telling people about it. If your community does not have one, make up a celebration or festival.

A Tradition or Celebration

name _____

Name of tradition or celebration: _____

Why is it celebrated or recognized?	
What happens at the tradition or celebration?	
Who takes part?	
When does it take place?	
Where does it take place?	

Early Settlers Activities

Activity Idea 1: Introduction to the idea of settlement

Approach the idea of settlement by talking to students about their own experiences of moving to a new home, school, town or country.

On chart paper or chalkboard put the following headings and list students' responses.

- ❖ Who decided to make the move?
- ❖ What kind of feeling did you have about it?
- ❖ What did you decide to take with you?
- ❖ What did you have to leave behind?

Other discussion questions may include:
- ❖ How did you travel to your new home?
- ❖ How long did the trip take?
- ❖ What was the trip like?
- ❖ What did you think of your new home?
- ❖ Were there any changes you had to make? (for example learn to speak English)

Activity 2: A New Life for Early Settlers

When most early settlers arrived in their new country, they still had a very long and hard journey to their new land. Journeys were made by foot or by cart. The number of supplies early settlers brought with them depended upon on their ability to afford them and to carry them. Here are some examples of supplies that early settlers brought with them.

• dishes	• cutlery	• rope	• kettle	• pail
• pots	• table	• hammer	• seed	• flour
• blankets	• candles	• ax	• spade	• hoe

The physical environment was a challenge for the early settlers because of the cold, and other conditions. It was important that they were prepared. The first tasks early settlers did when coming to their new land was to build some sort of shelter, clear the land for planting and to prepare for winter. This was all very hard backbreaking work.

- ❖ Which items were the most important on the supplies list? Explain your thinking.

- ❖ Why do you think it was necessary for early settlers to begin preparing for winter upon their arrival?

- ❖ How do you think life would be different for early settlers if they came to live in a warmer climate?

Early Settlers Activities

Activity Idea 3: Life Of An Early Settler

Talk with students about how the life of settlers was difficult. Things you may bring up include:

- farming accidents
- illness
- drought
- hunger

- loneliness
- winter cold
- crop diseases
- wild animals

Ask students what characteristics early settlers needed to have for a successful life in their new home. Have students explain their thinking. Teachers may wish to have students make a web of their ideas.

Have students write a letter of encouragement to a newly arrived early settler.

Activity 4: Comparing Life Back Then to Modern Days

Use the T-chart to compare life back in pioneer times to modern days. Comparisons can be done as a whole group, small group or independently:

Topics for comparison may include:

- early pioneer village and a modern town
- school
- types of occupations
- a day in the life of a grown up or child
- types of transportation
- homes
- finding food
- clothing

Activity 5: Early Settlers Worked Together

A "bee" was a type of work party where settlers got together to complete a difficult task that could only be done by a group of people. Tasks included making a quilt or building a home.

Organize a class "bee." Decide as a class what task to take on as a whole group. Some example include: cleaning up the school yard, creating a class art project, or raising money for a special trip. Once the task has been accomplished, hold a class celebration.

Activity 6: Early Settler Life Mural

Create a class mural composed of different panels that showed life in pioneer times. Panels may include the journey to their new home, clearing the land and building shelter, school time, the village etc.

Early Settlers

The first people to live in Canada were the Aboriginal people. They have lived here for thousands of years. Early settlers or pioneers are people who moved to Canada from other places to build homes and communities. Many of the early settlers were farmers, labourers, trades people and their families.

Early settlers came to live in Canada so they could have a better life. Some people came because they were very poor and could not find work where they lived. Some people came so they could freely practice their religion. Some people settled here because they did not like the way their home countries were governed.

Our Ancestors

Most Canadians have ancestors who decided to make Canada their home. Some Canadians have ancestors from early pioneer times. Some Canadians have grandparents or parents who moved to Canada. Some Canadians are newly arrived to Canada.

Brain Stretch:
- Create a family tree to show where your family originally comes from.
- Conduct a survey of your classmates and complete a graph to show where their families come from.

Aboriginal Peoples Helped With Food

Aboriginal peoples taught early settlers about having enough food. Many Aboriginal peoples were expert farmers and taught early settlers to best use the land.

For example, the women of the Iroquois nation taught the early settlers of Upper Canada how to grow tasty corn. They showed the early settlers how to choose good kernels for planting and how to make the soil rich with fish fertilizer. The ripe corn was then ground to make flour for cornmeal. The Iroquois also taught the early settlers how to plant other crops such as pumpkins, beans and squash.

Early Settlers: Making Butter

Make some delicious homemade butter and enjoy it on tasty fresh bread.

What you need:
- 1 cup whipping cream
- A wooden spoon
- small jar with lid
- a bowl
- bread

What you do:

1. Pour the whipping cream carefully into the jar.

2. Securely attach the jar lid and shake the jar vigouroulsy for at least 10 minutes. Take turns with other students.

3. As the jar is shaken, the whipping cream will separate into two parts. One part is buttermilk and the other part will be lumps of butter.

4. Next, carefully pour out the butter and buttermilk.

5. Rinse the butter with cold water.

6. Using the wooden spoon spread the butter on the bread and taste!

Comparing Back Then and Now

name _____

	Back Then	Now
Type of home		
How is your kept warm or cool?		
What do you use for lighting?		
Where do you cook?		
How do you preserve food?		
What kind of furniture and decorations does your home have?		

Comparing Back Then and Now

name _____

Comparing...	Back Then	Now

Aboriginal Peoples Contributions   name _____

Fill in the chart with information you have learned and researched.

Contribution	Example
Food	
Medicine	
Coping with Winter	

Comparing Meals

name _____

Meal	Back Then	Now
Breakfast	• Bread • Butter • Porridge	
Lunch	• Bread with butter and jam • Vegetables • Meat • Stew • Soup • Potatoes	
Dinner	• Fried Pork • Fish • Boiled Potatoes • Corn • Griddle Cakes • Dandelion Root Coffee	
Snacks	• Dried Apple Slices • Apple snow • Jerky • Pemmican • Fruit	
Desserts	• Pies • Baked Apples	

Meal Comparisons

name _____

1. Plan a menu as if you were living in pioneer times.

Breakfast	
Lunch	
Dinner	
Snack	

2. In pioneer times almost all food was grown, and homemade. Explain how you think grocery stores have changed life in modern days.

Comparing Family Chores

name _____

Family Member	Back Then	Now
Men and Older Boys	• Clearing the land • Cutting trees for lumber • Building a home • Removing big rocks from fields • Ploughing fields • Planting Crops • Harvesting Crops • Hunting • Shearing Sheep • Building Fences • Making Furniture • Digging wells	
Women and Older Girls	• Taking care of the children • Taking care of livestock • Making warm clothes, blankets • Preparing meals • Preserving and storing food • Planting Crops • Making Candles • Helping with the harvest	
Young Girls	• Helping take care of younger siblings • Feeding livestock • Washing Dishes	
Young Boys	• • Gathering firewood • Feeding and tending livestock • Helping with the harvest	

Pioneer Occupations

name _____

Trades people are people with special skills and have special tools. In pioneer times trades people would take on a child apprentice to teach them their trade. An apprentice was someone who learned a trade on the job. It usually took four to seven years of training to become a tradesman such as a blacksmith or a wainwright.

Blacksmith
A blacksmith's job was to fit oxen and horses with iron shoes. Iron shoes kept the hooves of these working animals from wearing away. The blacksmith also made iron tools like hoes, rakes, spades, scythes, and sickles. Other items the blacksmith crafted included sleigh runners, plow, nails, knives, and even guns.

Wainwright
Wainwrights built carriages. They built the top part of carriages, wagons sleighs and coaches using hardwoods such as oak, and elm. Wainwrights then hired other tradesmen like wheelwrights, blacksmiths, painters and woodworkers to complete the rest of the carriage.

Wheelwright
Wheelwrights crafted many sizes of wheels for carriages, wagons, carts, and wheelbarrows. Wheels were made with wooden hubs, spokes and rim. Then an iron ring called a tire was put around the outer part of the wheel to make it sturdy.

Cooper
The cooper in the village was the person who made barrels and kegs to store liquids and dry items. A coop is a kind of wooden container. Coopers also crafted household items like pails, buckets, butter churns and washtubs.

Shoemaker
Did you know the foot shapes that shoemakers carved were called lasts? The shoemaker used a last to help shape a piece of leather into a boot or shoe. Lasts came in three sizes: small, medium and large. Usually shoemakers made a child's pair of shoes a bit big, so that a child could grow into them. To make the shoes fit; rags would be stuffed into their shoes.

Pioneer Occupations

Harness Maker

Did you know harness makers were also called saddle makers? A harness maker was someone who carefully crafted leather harnesses and saddles for large animals like cows and horses.

If you lived in pioneer times, what occupation would you want to do? Explain your thinking.

_____

_____

_____

_____

_____

_____

_____

_____

_____

_____

_____

_____

_____

_____

_____

Create a _job wanted_ poster. Make sure you include:
- **The name of occupation**
- **Skills needed**
- **Characteristics needed to do the occupation**
- **Who to contact about the job.**

The Growth of Pioneer Villages

Pioneer villages were usually built on land near a lake or river.   This is because water was the easiest way to travel and to carry heavy supplies. Water was very important to the pioneers. Water was used for many things such as for drinking, cooking and washing.

People worked together to dam a nearby river and build a millpond. The flowing water from the millpond turned a water well and provided power to run a gristmill or sawmill. A gristmill ground wheat and other grains into flour. A sawmill sawed logs into wooden planks or boards. Some settlers got jobs at a mill. Other setters came to live nearby the mill.

Once a mill was built, new businesses such as the general store, blacksmith and tannery started up. The mill and these businesses attracted more people to live in the new village. A community church and school were built when there were enough people.

Brain Stretch:
- Create a map of a pioneer village.

Health

During pioneer times there were few doctors and hospitals. When settlers got sick or injured they were usually cared for at home.

Pioneers did not know the importance of washing their hands. Many pioneers believed that bathing too much washed away body oils that kept them from getting diseases.

Honey was used by pioneers to soothe sore throats and coughs. Honey was mixed with hot water, and lemon. Honey was also used as a salve for cuts and scrapes.

When pioneers had a toothache they would visit a blacksmith. A blacksmith would pull the tooth out with a pair of tongs. Pulling out a tooth was very painful because there was no freezing or painkillers for the person.

Brain Stretch:
- Write a letter to a person in pioneer times explaining how taking care of our health in the modern days has changed.

School Time

by _____

School was very different in pioneer times than now. Children went to school in a one room schoolhouse. All the grades were in the same class. Students sat on wooden benches at narrow tables. In the centre of the room was a large boxwood stove or fireplace to heat the room. If there was no village school, children learned what they could from their parents.

A male teacher was called a schoolmaster. A female teacher was called a schoolmistress. The families of all the students paid the teacher's salary. Sometimes teachers were paid with money or given things grown on a farm like a bag of flour, vegetables or a cured ham. Sometimes teachers lived with a student's family for a period of time as payment.

Teachers were very strict. If students misbehaved they were whacked on the hands with a birch rod or stick.
Students were taught reading, writing and math. In early schools, students had a slate board and slate to complete their work. Later on, students wrote on paper using a quill pen. A quill pen was made using a large goose feather. The end of the quill was sharpened with a knife to make a point to dip into ink.

Brain Stretch:

1. How is school different in the modern days? Explain your thinking.

_____

_____

_____

_____

_____

_____

_____

_____

_____

Early Settlers Project Outline by _____

This research project is about:

_____

Location

Village Life
What were their villages like?

Early Settlers Project Outline

by _____

Homes

What kind of homes did they have?

Food

What did they do for food?

Early Settlers Project Outline

by _____

Transportation
What did they do for transportation?

Tools
What kind of tools did they use?

Early Settlers Project Outline   by _____

Interesting Facts
Write about other interesting facts you have learned.

Editing Checklist:

I have a topic sentence for each section.   _____

I wrote complete sentences.   _____

I checked for capitals and periods.   _____

I checked with the teacher and I am ready to complete a good copy.

Teacher's signature

Comparing Buildings

name _____

Complete the chart.

Buildings In A Pioneer Village	Buildings In Your Community:

Brain Stretch:
1. **On a separate piece of paper, compare and contrast.**
   - How are the buildings the same?

   - How are the buildings different?

2. Complete a Venn diagram to compare buildings back then and now.

An Advertisement Poster

name _____

Create a poster to attract people to come and live in Canada.
For a top quality advertisement, make sure to include:

    1. Two reasons to come live in Canada.

    2. A detailed picture with neat printing.

What I think I know...

What I wonder about...

New Vocabulary

New Word	Definition

Non-Fiction Reports

Encourage students to read informational text and to recall what they have read in their own words. Provide a theme related space or table in your with subject related materials and artifacts including, books, tapes, posters, posters and magazines etc.

Have students explore the different sections usually found in a non-fiction book:

The Title Page: The book title and the author's name.

The Table of Contents: The title of each chapter, what page it starts on and where you can find specific information.

The Glossary: The meaning of special words used in the book.

The Index: The ABC list of specific topics you can find in the book.

Next, discuss criteria of a good research project.

It should include:

- a presentation board or other medium.
- proper grammar and punctuation, for example, capitals and periods.
- print size that can be read from far away.
- neat colouring and detailed drawings.

Oral Reports

Encourage students to talk about what they have learned or to make a presentation to the class. Here are tips to discuss with students.

- Use your best voice, speak slowly, and make sure your voice is loud so everyone can hear.
- Look at your audience and try not to sway.
- Introduce your topic in an interesting way (Riddle, or Question).
- Choose the most important things to tell.
- Point to pictures, a model, or diorama, as you present.

Blooms Taxonomy In The Classroom

Knowledge: (recall)

- *Activities:* match, describe, identify, name, select, and define.
- *Products:* time line, a facts chart, make a list
- *Ask questions such as:* What are the definitions of _____?
  Can you name the _____?

Comprehension: (understanding)

- *Activities:* explain, predict, summarize, classify, and sort.
- *Products:* cartoon strip, draw a picture
- *Ask questions such as:* Why do you think…?
  What are the differences?
  Explain your thinking with an example

Application: (using information)

- *Activities:* rearrange, solve problems, modify, and demonstrate.
- *Products:* mural, make a scrapbook, diorama, dress us as___
- *Ask questions such as:* What questions would you ask?
  Can you group by characteristics such as?
  Could this have happened in _____?

Analysis: (studying the components)

- *Activities:* order, estimate, subdivide, infer, separate
- *Products:* family tree, construct a graph to show the information, prepare a report
- *Ask questions such as:* Can you explain what must have happened when ___?
  How is _____similar to _____?
  What are some of the problems of _____?

Synthesis: (creating a whole from parts)

- *Activities:* design, create, compose, combine, rearrange, construct
- *Products:* Design a t-shirt, write a story
- *Ask questions such as:* Draw _____.
  Create a model that shows _____.
  How could you make ____?

Evaluation: (making judgements)

- *Activities:* justify, categorize, conclude, support, compare
- *Products: write a letter, make a booklet and convince others of your ideas*
- *Ask questions like:* What solution did you like best? Why?
  What was the best/worst thing about _____?
  Which ____ did you like? Why?

name _____

Write about your stamp.

_____

_____

Write A letter

Dear _____

_____

_____

_____

_____

_____

_____

_____

_____

_____

_____

_____

Your friend,

_____

A Flip Book

name _____

Make a flip book about your topic of study using outline pages. Fold the sheet along the dotted line. Next, cut the sheet along the dark solid lines. Answer the question on the outside page, and draw a picture to go with it on the inside page.

Compare and Contrast

Compare to look at what things are the **same**.
Contrast to look what things are **different**.
Find two things, people, events or ideas to compare and contrast.

Compare
How are they the **same?**

Contrast
How are they the **different?**

A Venn Diagram About _____

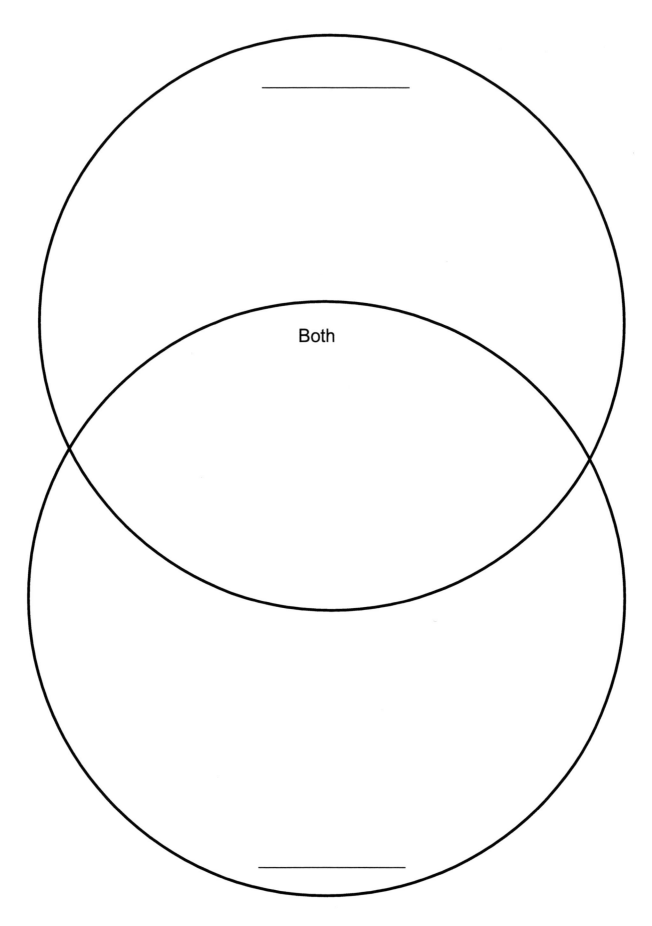

Both

A Web About _____

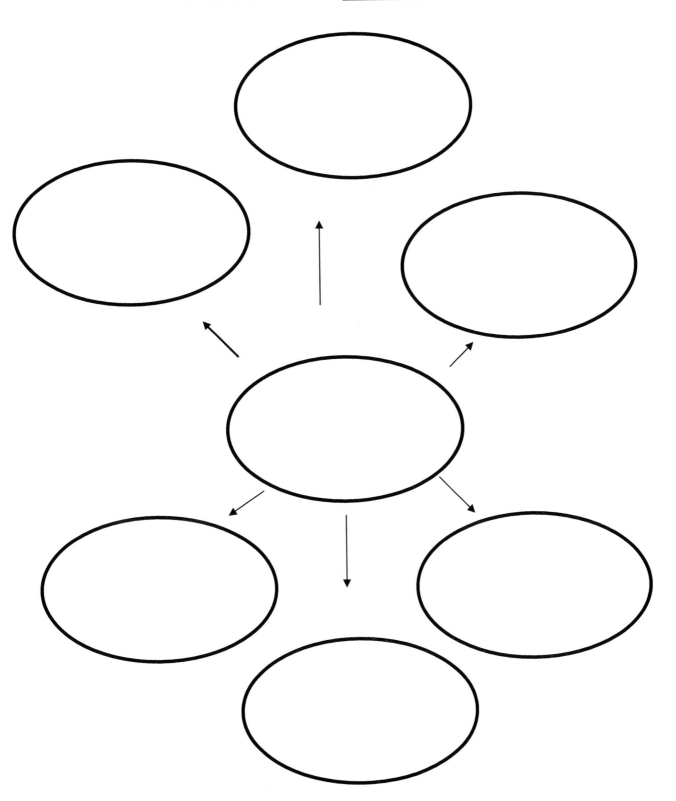

Comparison Chart

name _____

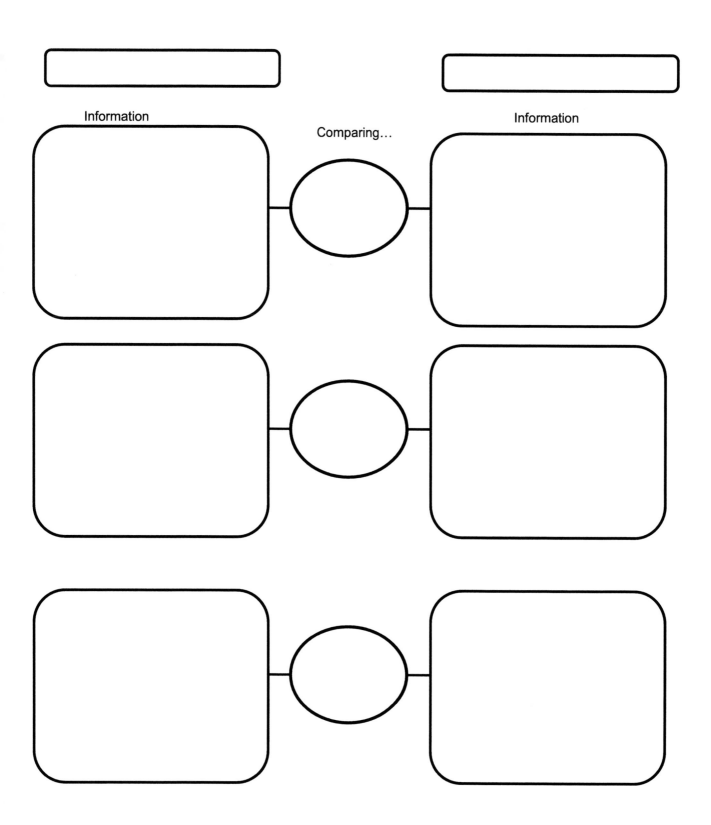

Information

Comparing…

Information

Conduct A Survey

name _____

This is a graph about _____

_____

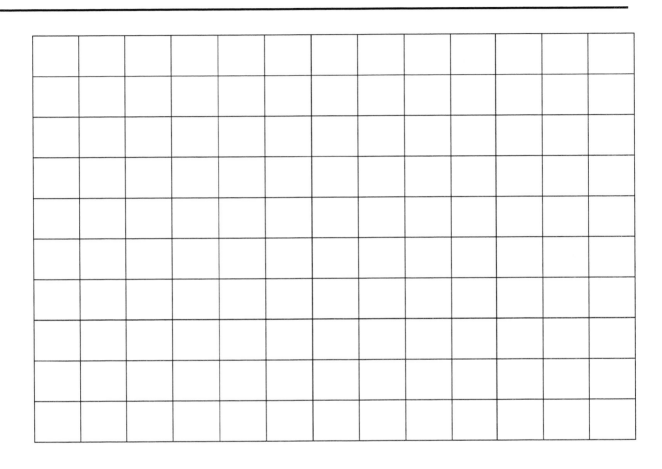

_____

By looking at the graph I learned that:

_____

_____

_____

_____

A POST CARD

Write a postcard to a friend and state why your community is special.

Front of Postcard

Back of the Postcard

To:

_____

_____

_____

_____

A T-Chart About _____

What I wonder ...

name _____

This is a map of _____

N
W ⊕ E
S

Legend

A comparison of _____

Comparing…..		
Who?		
What?		
Where?		
When?		
How?		

Write a News Story

Pretend you are a newspaper reporter and a write a news story.

- A sports story
- A community event
- An interview with a community leader
- A historical event

Here are the parts of an article.

- The **HEADLINE** names the story.

- The **BYLINE** names the author.

- The **BEGINNING** tells the reader the most important idea.

- The **MIDDLE** gives details about the story.

- The **ENDING** gives the reader an idea to remember.

Newspaper Article Checklist:

Grammar and Style

❑   I used my neatest writing and included a clear title.

❑   I included a colourful picture.

❑   I checked for spelling.

❑   I used interesting words.

❑   I checked for capitals, periods, commas, and question marks.

Content

❑   I have a **HEADLINE** that names the story.

❑   I have a **BYLINE** that shows my name as the author.

❑   I have a **BEGINNING** that gives the most important facts.

❑   I have a **MIDDLE** part that tells details about the story.

❑   I have an **ENDING** that gives the reader an idea to remember.

Diorama Scene

A diorama is a small version of a real life scene. Create a diorama about a topic you are studying.

What you need:
Here are some materials that you might like to use to make your diorama:

- cardboard box, pizza box or shoe box
- found materials like yarn, or tissue paper rolls
- construction paper
- tissue paper,
- paint
- glue
- scissors

What you do:

STEP 1: Choose a diorama stage like a cardboard box or shoe box.

STEP 2: Paint or draw and colour a background for your diorama.

STEP 3: Use the diorama outlines to draw and colour things to help create your diorama. Add other details for your diorama using different materials.

STEP 4: Write about your diorama.

Diorama Outlines

Use these outlines to help create a diorama.

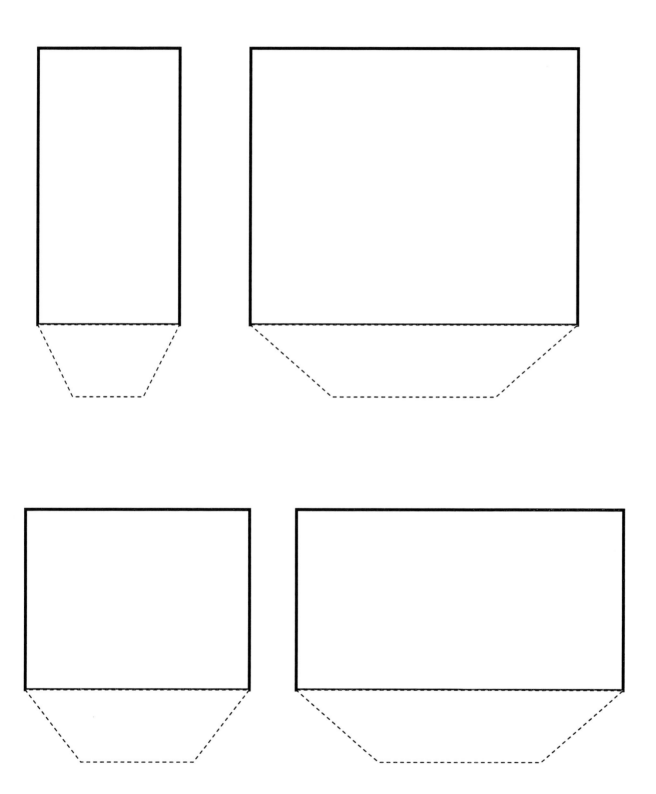

Diorama Outlines

Use these outlines to help create a diorama.

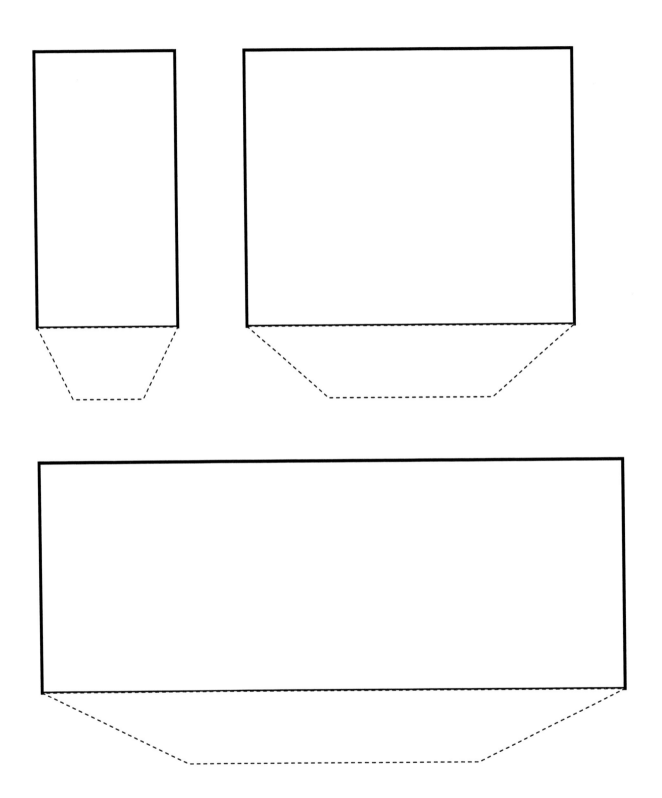

A Word Search About

_____

Create a word search and share it with your classmates.

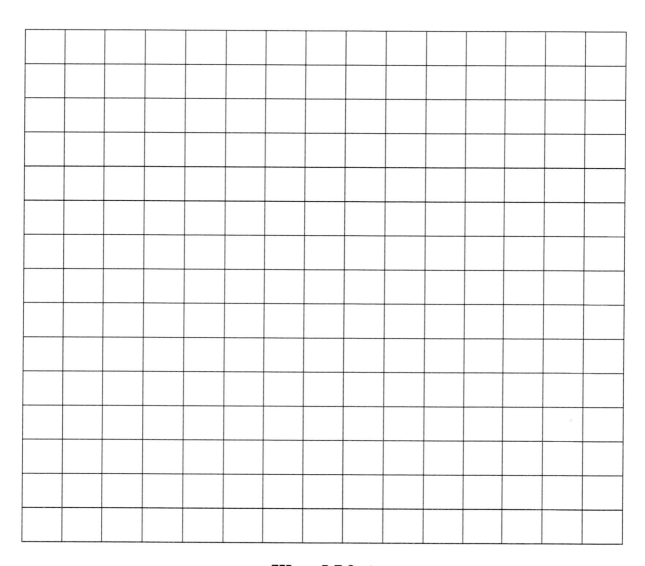

Word List

Thinking About My Work!

name _____

I am proud of _____

_____

I want to learn more about _____

_____

I need to work on _____

I will do better by _____

Thinking About My Work!

name _____

I am proud of _____

_____

I want to learn more about _____

_____

I need to work on _____

I will do better by _____

Map Making Checklist

name _____

Organization and Neatness • My work is neat and has details. • My features can be clearly read. • I have a title for my map.	
Map Legend • I have a complete map legend.	
Scale • The features are drawn to scale.	
Spelling • I checked for spelling.	

Map Making Checklist

name _____

Organization and Neatness • My work is neat and has details. • My features can be clearly read. • I have a title for my map.	
Map Legend • I have a complete map legend.	
Scale • The features are drawn to scale.	
Spelling • I checked for spelling.	

Map Making Rubric

Student name_____

	Level 1	Level 2	Level 3	Level 4
Organization and Neatness	Few of the labels or features can be clearly read.	Some of the labels or features can be clearly read.	Most of the labels or features can be clearly read.	Almost all of the labels or features can be clearly read.
Map Legend	The legend is missing or difficult to read.	The legend contains an incomplete set of symbols.	The legend contains a set of symbols.	The legend contains a thorough set of symbols.
Scale	Less than half of the features on the map are drawn to scale.	More than half of the features on the map are drawn to scale.	Most of the features on the map are drawn to scale.	Almost all of the features on the map are drawn to scale.
Spelling	Less than half of the words on the map are spelled correctly.	More than half of the words on the map are spelled correctly.	Most of the words on the map are spelled correctly.	Almost all of the words on the map are spelled correctly.

Teacher Comments:

_____
_____
_____
_____

Student Participation Rubric

Level	Student Participation Descriptor
Level 4	Student consistently contributes to class discussions and activities by offering ideas and asking questions.
Level 3	Student usually contributes to class discussions and activities by offering ideas and asking questions.
Level 2	Student sometimes contributes to class discussions and activities by offering ideas and asking questions.
Level 1	Student rarely contributes to class discussions and activities by offering ideas and asking questions.

Understanding Of Concepts Rubric

Level	Understanding of Concepts Descriptor
Level 4	Student shows a thorough understanding of all or almost all concepts and consistently gives appropriate and complete explanations independently. No teacher support is needed.
Level 3	Student shows a good understanding of most concepts and usually gives complete or nearly complete explanations. Infrequent teacher support is needed.
Level 2	Student shows a satisfactory understanding of most concepts and sometimes gives appropriate, but incomplete explanations. Teacher support is sometimes needed.
Level 1	Student shows little of understanding of concepts and rarely gives complete explanations. Intensive teacher support is needed.

Communication Of Concepts Rubric

Level	Communication of Concepts Descriptor
Level 4	Student consistently communicates with clarity and precision in written and oral work. Student consistently uses appropriate terminology and vocabulary.
Level 3	Student usually communicates with clarity and precision in written and oral work. Student usually uses appropriate terminology and vocabulary.
Level 2	Student sometimes communicates with clarity and precision in written and oral work. Student sometimes uses appropriate terminology and vocabulary.
Level 1	Student rarely communicates with clarity and precision in written and oral work. Student rarely uses appropriate terminology and vocabulary.

Class Evaluation List

Student Name	Class Participation	Understanding of Concepts	Communication of Concepts	Overall Evaluation

Social Studies Star!

_____

GREAT WORK !

Quality Worker!

_____

Way to go!

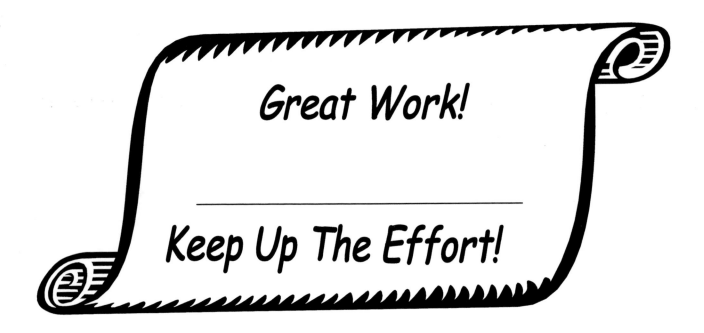

Great Work!

_____

Keep Up The Effort!

Social Studies

Award

_____